The Wild West

The Way the American West Was Lost and Won, 1845-1893

AN EDITED TRANSCRIPT

CHANNEL FOUR TELEVISION

Present-day Historians and Commentators

Stephen E. Ambrose is Boyd Professor of History at the University of New Orleans, Lousiana, and the author of numerous books on American history.

Charlotte Black Elk – a descendant of Black Elk, the famous Oglala Lakota holy man – is an attorney at Pine Ridge, South Dakota.

Dee Brown is best known for his epic *Bury My Heart at Wounded Knee*, and is the author of more than 25 other books on American history and the West.

John Carter is curator of photographs at the Nebraska State Historical Society.

Ian Frazier is a contributing editor of the *New Yorker* magazine.

Mike Her Many Horses is an historian and former executive director of the Oglala Sioux Tribal Council at Pine Ridge, South Dakota.

Alvin M. Josephy, Jr is the author of numerous award-winning magazine articles and books on Indian affairs and US and Western history. He is also currently president of the Western History Association, and chairman of the Board of Trustees of the National Museum of the American Indian, part of the Smithsonian Institution in Washington, DC.

Thomas McGuane is the author of many novels and collections of essays concerning contemporary western American life and culture, including *Ninety-two in the Shade, Panama, The Bushwacked Piano, The Sporting Club, Nobody's Angel, Something to be Desired* and *Nothing but Blue Skies*.

Marie Not Help Him is great-great-granddaughter of Dewey Beard, a Minneconjou Sioux who was a survivor of both the battle of Little Big Horn and the massacre at Wounded Knee.

Mardell Plainfeather, a member of the Crow tribe, was a Plains Indian historian at the Little Big Horn National Monument. Currently she is Chief Ranger at the Fort Smith National Historic Site Museum in Arkansas.

Robert M. Utley, the author of numerous books, specialises in the history of the transMississippi frontier of the American West.

PROLOGUE

My father told of a fearful dream. He said: 'I dreamt I saw the greatest emigration that has yet been through our country. I looked North and South and East and West, and saw nothing but dust, and I heard a great weeping. I saw women crying, and my men shot down by the white people. Oh, my dear children! You may all think it is only a dream, but I feel that it will come to pass.'

Sarah Winnemucca, 1845

Fewer than 20,000 white Americans lived west of the Mississippi River in 1845. The western third of the continent was a foreign wilderness, to which white Americans had little or no legal claim. Buffalo by the millions blackened the vast windswept plains. Hundreds of thousands of Native Americans in half a hundred tribes made their homes across the prairies and mountains of the Far West.

Americans had been dreaming of the West for centuries when, in 1845, John L. O'Sullivan, a New York newspaper editor, uttered a fateful declaration: 'It is our manifest destiny to overspread the continent allotted by Providence for the free development of our yearly multiplying millions.' One year later, the nation exploded westward to fulfill that destiny, and the most troubling and transformative episode in American history had begun.

Between 1845 and 1893, the American West was lost and won. The vast continent that Thomas Jefferson was sure would take 1000 years to settle and subdue was wound with ribbons of iron and wire- and brought within the dominion of the United States. Along the way, the lives of hundreds of thousands of Native Americans were violently disrupted and all but destroyed.

We gave them forestclad mountains and valleys full of game, and in return, what did they give our warriors and our women? Rum and trinkets and a grave.

Tecumseh

The West was a battleground – the place where the European sense of the force of order met the forces of chaos, where the handiwork of man met the handiwork of nature ... [White] people saw the landscape as a daunting, conquerable environment, and unfortunately, the people who were living on the landscape didn't have that sense.

They were comfortable with the rhythms of nature as they existed, that didn't need to be parsed up and organised and possessed, owned or controlled by a human being.

John Carter

As the nation surged west, the struggle between Native Americans and European whites, begun four centuries before, came to a climax out on the Great Plains. In part, the war was about the land itself. But it was also about incompatible visions of America – and about the promise, and the sorrow, of the American dream.

"Millions are marching at once towards the same horizon. Their language, their religion, their manners differ; their object is the same. Fortune has been promised them somewhere in the West, and to the West they go to find it."
ALEXIS DE TOCQUEVILLE 1805-1859

Left: Yellowstone, Wyoming as it appeared in 1871, the year before President Grant made it the first US national park – a 'pleasuring ground for the people'.

Opposite page: Federal commissioners and Sioux at Fort Laramie, Wyoming to sign the Treaty of 1868, which created the Great Sioux Reservation.

CHAPTER ONE

'WESTWARD HO'

1845-1861

There were 10 million Native Americans on the continent when the first whites arrived in the 1490s – seeking wealth and redemption and armed with the Christian commandment to subdue the Earth. Over the next three centuries, 90 per cent of the original population was wiped out by the diseases, famine and warfare imported by the whites.

By 1840, all the eastern tribes had been subdued, annihilated – or forcibly removed to Indian territory, west of the Mississippi.

These tribes cannot exist surrounded by our settlements and in continual contact with our citizens. They have neither the intelligence, the industry, the moral habits, nor the desire of improvement. They must necessarily yield to the force of circumstance and, ere long, disappear.
President Andrew Jackson

Now only 360,000 Native Americans remained on the continent. Most of them made their homes in the endless western territories beyond Missouri: a 'permanent Indian domain' where Native Americans could dwell free from white encroachment.

Whites looked upon the transMississippi West as the Great American Desert . . . Here was a place that white agrarians would never covet. Indians could live there for ever, undisturbed by white contamination, and there would be no conflict between the races. The separating line was defined as the permanent Indian frontier. And this was supposed to be, for ever, the United States Indian policy.
Robert Utley

Few besides fur traders and mountain men were willing to risk the gruelling 2000-mile journey across Indian country to the Pacific – until 1843, when the 'permanent Indian frontier' began to crumble. Land hunger in the east was already rising when the explorer and promoter John C. Fremont published a breathtaking revelation: ordinary families in covered wagons could cross the Rocky Mountains at South Pass in Wyoming.

That spring, 1000 pioneers stepped off into the wilderness at Independence, Missouri, bound for the promised lands of Oregon and California. By 1846, the fever for expansion had propelled the Mormons west towards the Great Salt Lake, forced England to cede Oregon and brought on a war with Mexico over Texas, California and the entire South-west. By 1848, the nation's western boundary had been pushed all the way to the Pacific, and more than two million square miles had been added to the United States.

———◆———

No one was prepared for what was about to happen in the rugged mountains of upper California. On 24 January 1848, a mechanic named James Marshall was inspecting a sawmill in the Sierra Nevada when he saw something glittering in the bottom of the stream. 'Boys,' he said, 'I believe I've found a gold mine.'

Marshall's discovery set in motion one of the most frantic stampedes for instant wealth in history. Thousands of men from around the country and around the globe converged on

"Soon there will come from the rising sun a different kind of man from any you have yet seen. They will bring with them a book that will teach you everything. After that, the world will fall to pieces."
SPOKAN

Above: Alfred Fredericks' version of the purchase of Manhattan from the Indians by the Dutchman, Peter Minuit, in 1626. By 1800, 90 per cent of the Eastern Indians had disappeared.

Opposite page: Westward, the Course of Empire Takes Its Way: *Emanuel Leutze's 1861 painting of American pioneers heading west, in the rotunda of the US Capitol.*

SALT LAKE CITY IN 1850.

Salt Lake City, Utah, in 1850, three years after it was founded by the Mormons.

Indians Watching the Wagon Train: *painting by Oscar Berninghaus (1874–1952).*

California. It was said that the rivers and streams ran with gold, that the average miner made $1000 a day, that one man had dug up $9000 in less than 24 hours.

The California Gold Rush changed the destiny of the continent, almost overnight. In less than a year, the population of San Francisco jumped from 429 to more than 25,000, and just two years after James Marshall's discovery, California entered the Union as the 31st state. But the Gold Rush did more than hasten settlement of the Far West coastline. It also sent hundreds of thousands of white Americans streaming over the Great Plains and out into the permanent Indian domain. Watching the endless stream of wagon trains moving west, Native Americans began to speak of emigrating eastward – unable to believe that any whites could be left there

Before the first non-Indians began to come out here, we had control over, or access to, about 60 million acres of land. It ranged from mountains to plains to rivers, and so we had a huge environment to deal with. The land could only support so many people in a region, so you had a leader who had to have knowledge of the environment – where game was, where you could procure plants for food, fish, good drinking water, firewood . . . We knew where we were going, we knew where we had to procure food and the things that sustained us. It was an annual journey that we made over the course of the seasons so that we could live.

Mike Her Many Horses

No one else has ever experienced anything to compare with being a Sioux Indian in the 1840s, with those magnificent horses, and this marvellous sweep of grasslands and immense herds of buffalo, and

the opportunity to ride and to hunt and to live freely. The openness of Indian life, the absence of geographical constraint, the absence of political restraint – they were the freest people the world has ever known.

Stephen Ambrose

Of all the tribes on the northern Plains, the seven divisions of the Teton Lakota – or Sioux, as their enemies called them – were the most numerous, the most powerful and the most recently arrived. With their allies, the Cheyenne and the Arapaho, they roamed the high plains from the Missouri River to the Big Horn Mountains, vying for control of the rich buffalo ranges with the Pawnee, the Shoshoni and their arch-enemies, the Crow. Many of these tribes spoke different languages, followed different customs and differed widely in their attitudes towards the whites. What united them was their attitude towards the land.

The Indians saw the land as being a part of them, that they were a part of the land. They never claimed ownership, and I don't think that there was ever a time that they put up fences. When the wasichu *came, it was that the land was theirs, and they had papers that proved that it was theirs. And that's the difference.*

Marie Not Help Him

By 1850, the crush of gold seekers streaming west over the Oregon and Santa Fe trails had created a crisis for Native Americans. Each spring and summer, endless trains of covered wagons rumbled west over the Holy Road – bringing devastating diseases, devouring timber and grass, and scaring away the buffalo. Tribes that had once traded amiably with the whites began to beg and steal from the emigrants – or to exact tribute in exchange for the right to pass through their country unmolested.

In 1851, hoping to find a solution to the 'Indian problem', the government called all the tribes on the northern Plains into Fort Laramie, a remote military outpost on the Oregon Trail.

Treaty negotiators offered the tribes $50,000 a year, plus guns, if they would keep away from the emigrant trails and confine themselves to designated tracts of land. Although no one used the term, it was a first step towards a reservation system.

No worse mechanism for regulating the relations between the United States and the Indian tribes could have been conceived than the treaty. No Indian chief could speak for all of his people, or

guarantee that what he had agreed to in the treaty was going to be carried out by his people. That simply was not Indian political organisation.
Robert Utley

Some leaders signed the Treaty of 1851, but most knew it would be impossible to comply with its terms. Year after year, tension along the overland trails mounted. Petty violence against the wagon trains increased, and more and more soldiers were sent west to defend the trails.

Thirty-five years of bitter warfare between the United States Army and the Lakota Sioux began with a dispute over a cow. On 18 August 1854, not far from Fort Laramie, a warrior named High Forehead stole a lame cow from a Mormon wagon train Conquering Bear, an amiable Lakota leader, offered to replace the animal with two of his own, but the inexperienced officers at Fort Laramie insisted on High Forehead's surrender. The next day, Lieutenant John Grattan, a West Point graduate eager to 'crack it to the Sioux', marched 31 men and two mountain howitzers into Conquering Bear's camp.

While hundreds of armed Lakota warriors looked on, the negotiations quickly broke down. Grattan's interpreter, who was drunk, shouted obscenities at the Indians. Conquering Bear repeatedly refused to surrender High Forehead, who was a guest in his village. Grattan's patience snapped, and he ordered his men to fire into the village at point blank range. Nine bullets ripped into Conquering Bear, who fell to the ground, mortally wounded. There was a moment's silence. Then hundreds of enraged Lakota warriors swarmed down on the company of white men, killing them all and pounding Grattan's face to pulp with rocks.

Had the Lakota followed up their victory that day, they might have overrun Fort Laramie and closed the Oregon Trail. But they could agree on no concerted action. Two days later, while terrified whites huddled inside the fort, the Lakota broke camp and headed north.

One year later, the US Army came west to punish the Sioux. On September 1855, 600 soldiers stormed into Nebraska and fell on a village on Blue Water Creek, killing 86 men, capturing 70 women and children and burning the village to the ground.

The Lakota were stunned by the disaster. Never before had an entire village been destroyed by white soldiers. Never before had Lakota women and children been killed by whites. Many bands agreed to submit to white authority and permit white travel on the

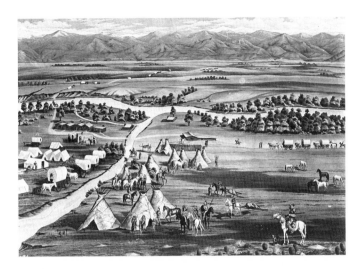

Oregon Trail. Others drifted south – and north: up into the buffalo ranges of the Powder River country, far away from the white invaders along the Platte.

———◆———

From a hilltop overlooking the Lakota camp, a 13-year-old Oglala boy named Curly had watched the massacre unfold. Shocked by what he had seen, he went into the Sand Hills of Nebraska to seek a vision. For two days, he fasted, staring into the sky. On the third day, he fell into a trance, and began to dream.

He saw his own horse approaching, a naked warrior on its back, white spots of hail painted on his body, a white streak of lightning painted on his face. The horse and rider floated in mid-air. A red-backed hawk flew over his head, screaming. Bullets and arrows flew all around the warrior, but nothing harmed him.

Later, after the boy had killed his first man in combat, his father helped him understand the meaning of his vision: He would never be killed on the field of battle. He was to look after his people, to defend them from the white invaders, to become a great leader. And he was to receive a new name: Crazy Horse.

Among the Lakota people . . . we have a great tradition of shedding the blood . . . that the people will live. And Crazy Horse was someone

Left: Denver, Colorado, in 1859, when it was a stopping place for trappers, traders and Indians. A year later, the town boomed during the gold rush to Pike's Peak.

Panning for gold in California. The various gold rushes in the western United States did more to speed the demise of the Native Americans than anything else.

Pioneers in a wagon train passing through Echo Canyon, Utah, 1866/67. Some of them settled here – see page 23.

'Pioneers' in a covered wagon – a photograph posed in 1921, when quite a few of those who had ventured West would still have been alive.

who belonged to warrior society. It went beyond marksmanship, beyond being fearless. It had to do more with someone saying, 'So that my people will live, I will sacrifice myself.'

Charlotte Black Elk

Peace of a kind returned to the Lakota, but by the late 1850s, Native Americans across the West could see that a great change was coming upon them. Once the whites had merely passed through their lands. Soon they would be coming to settle, and once they did, they would never go away.

I think a lot of it has to do with its blankness. Before the European peoples who settled the country . . . reached the Plains, they had geographic environments that could remind them of where they had come from. But when they got to the Big Sky, when they got to the empty land of the West, they didn't really have any hint as to where

they were and what this was, so that now they really had to invent themselves as Americans. That's why, to me, the West has always been the laboratory of identity for Americans.

Ian Frazier

Although the men and women who settled the West went for many different reasons, 'they agreed,' as one emigrant wrote, 'on one general object – that of bettering their condition.' Some longed, one prospector said, to expunge 'the detested sin of being poor'. Others were fired by utopian dreams – 'To forsake all,' a Mormon pioneer recorded, 'and build up the Kingdom of God.' But of all the dreams that drove people West, none would be more powerfully transforming than the dream of owning land.

In its broadest sense, the American dream was one of unbridled promise – that with the force of will and a little bit of energy, you could make anything out of anything. In a narrower sense, the dream had to do with land itself. There's something sacred to Western tradition about the association of human beings and the land. The call of the land was a siren call that was irresistible to large numbers of people.

John Carter

There seemed to be nothing to see: no fences, no creeks or trees, no hills or fields. There was nothing but land: not a country at all, but the material out of which countries are made.

Willa Cather

The men and women who would one day push out on to the Great Plains faced a beautiful, cruel and unforgiving landscape. They were mostly ordinary people, eager to make something extraordinary of the land and of themselves. It took all the courage they could muster.

Chatfield quite sick with scarlet fever. A calf took sick and died before breakfast. Last one of our oxen: he dropped dead in the yoke. I could hardly help shedding tears. Yesterday my eighth child was born.

Amelia Knight

250 miles to the nearest post office; 100 miles to wood; 20 miles to water; 6 inches to hell. Gone to live with the wife's folks.

Anonymous

But for all those who gave up and got out, there were those who persevered, seeing in the West something else, something stark and glorious. Often it was just the land itself.

To mount a horse and gallop over prairies, completely losing one's self in vast and illimitable space, as silent as lonely, is to leave every petty care. In these grand wastes, one is truly alone with God. Oh, how I love the West!

Mrs Orsemus Boyd

When you see where they lived, when you see the little indentation in the hillside that was their dugout, and you realise a woman spent a winter there, and cooked, and cut pretty patterns out of newspapers to put on the windows trying to prettify . . . they're living in a hole in the ground in western Kansas. It's almost as if this is the place where courage is preserved.

Ian Frazier

On 3 April 1860, the first relay rider of the Pony Express streaked west out of St Joseph, Missouri, with 49 letters in his satchel. Just 19 months later, the last rider delivered the mail in San Francisco, and went looking for a new job. The Pony Express had been rendered instantly obsolete on 21 October 1861, when the first transcontinental telegraph message flashed between San Francisco and Washington DC. It had once taken five months for news to cross the continent. Now it took seconds

Within a very few decades, the land – which was once so expansive as to not be comprehendable by the minds of humans – was settled, peppered with towns, mapped, organised, broken up, parcelled out. The speed with which that transformation took place is difficult to imagine.

John Carter

Ten years after the Gold Rush, almost half a million Americans had flooded the Pacific Far West and thousands more had begun pushing into the interior. By 1858, President James Buchanan was predicting that the whole country, east and west, would soon be bound 'by a chain of Americans which could never be broken'. Less than three years later, Buchanan was proved disastrously wrong. As each new western territory came into the Union, the fateful question was raised: would the new state be slave or free?

From Missouri to Kansas and Nebraska and beyond, the debate over slavery erupted into bloodshed again and again. By 1861, the expanding nation had torn itself apart. The terrible civil war that ensued would only make life worse for Native Americans.

The outbreak of the Civil War changed the military equation in the West. Initially, the regular army left to go help fight the Civil War, but almost immediately they were replaced by large numbers of volunteer soldiers, far more than before the war and much better soldiers than the pre-war regulars. They were motivated young men with a very uncomplicated view of Indians. Many of them thought the answer to the Indian problem was simply extermination.

Robert Utley

By 1861, a new solution to the so-called 'Indian problem' had come to the fore. Wherever Native Americans occupied territory that emigrants wanted to cross, mine or cultivate, the government would use every means at its disposal to move them on to special colonies called 'reservations'. In exchange, Native Americans would receive annual cash stipends from the government and be taught how to become self-sufficient farmers.

It's hard to conceive of anything more offensive from the Indian point of view than the loss of freedom and the bonds that make them dependent upon the dole system, on rations, for life.

Robert Utley

In theory, reservations would provide a humane alternative to extermination – safe havens where Native Americans could be kept from the path of emigration, protected from whites and eventually civilised, Christianised and controlled. In reality, they brought rancid food, arid lands, plagues of cholera and whiskey, and corrupt Indian agents, who often cheated them out of their annuities, which often never came at all. Reservations, one agent said, were simply 'the legalised murder of a whole nation: expensive, vicious and inhumane'.

Freedom was taken from them. Freedom to think for themselves, freedom to hunt for themselves, freedom to provide for themselves, freedom to feed themselves. Everything was taken from them, and then it was turned around and they were hated because of it. In the name of progress.

Mardell Plainfeather

While the Civil War raged on in the east, the conflict between Native Americans and whites would come to a series of bloody confrontations out West – starting in 1862, in the gentle rolling hill country of southern Minnesota.

An advertisement for the Pony Express in July 1861. The mention of telegrams to Fort Kearney (now in Nebraska) was a sign that the horse-borne postal service was to have a short life.

CHAPTER TWO

WAR COMES TO THE PLAINS

1862-1865

Forces that would permanently transform the West were quietly set in motion in Washington DC in 1862, when Congress passed the Homestead Act, offering free land to anyone willing to go out and work it. Millions of Americans would take up the government's offer and push out into the vast empty spaces of the Great Plains. That same year, Abraham Lincoln signed into law the Pacific Railroad Act. Soon twin ribbons of steel were creeping east from Sacramento, California, and west from Council Bluffs, Iowa.

The white men are like the locusts when they fly so thick that the whole sky is a snowstorm. You may kill one – two – ten – and ten times ten will come to kill you. Count your fingers all day long and white men with guns in their hands will come faster than you can count. Little Crow

By August 1862, the 12,000 people crowded on to the Santee Sioux reservation in Minnesota had had enough. For years, they had backed down as emigrants pressed into their territory – giving up 26 million acres and receiving in return barren land and cash allotments that barely kept their families alive. Then, in 1861, cutworms had devastated their corn crop. They got through the winter on credit grudgingly extended by white merchants. But when their annual allotments failed to come that June, all credit was cut off at the government store 'If they are hungry,' the trader Andrew Myrick said, 'let them eat grass or their own dung.'

By August, the Santees were starving to death. Their 52-year-old leader Little Crow tried to warn the whites what was coming: 'We have waited a long time. We have no food, but here are stores, filled with food. We ask you: make some arrangement by which we can get food, or we will keep ourselves from starving.'

On Sunday, 17 August 1862, four Santee men went on a rampage, killing three white men and two women. At dawn the next day, Little Crow himself, who for years had counselled peace with the settlers, led a column of starving warriors on to the reservation, shouting, 'Kill the whites! Kill all the whites!'

'They came down upon us like the wind,' one survivor remembered. For six weeks, the Santees raged across the Minnesota countryside, looting storehouses, burning homesteads and farms and killing hundreds of settlers. One of the first to die was Andrew Myrick, his body mutilated, his mouth stuffed with grass.

You have no idea of the uncontrollable panic everywhere in this country. The most horrible massacres have been committed; children nailed alive to trees and houses; women violated and then disembowelled – everything that horrible ingenuity could devise.

General John Pope

It took six weeks for the Army to arrive, and two months more to put down the insurrection. Little Crow escaped, but by October, 2000 Santee warriors had surrendered or been captured. The Great Sioux Uprising – the bloodiest rebellion ever mounted against the reservation system – was over.

Some whites blamed the disaster on the corrupt Indian policy of the United States, but most Minnesotans cried out for vengeance: 307 Santee men were swiftly tried by military commission and condemned to death. The evidence against most of them was so weak that President Lincoln commuted the sentences of all but 38. They were hanged on the chilly morning of 26 December in Mankato, while a few whites taunted and jeered. Three innocent men were accidentally put to death when their names were confused with those of the condemned.

Six months later, a farmer near Hutchinson, Minnesota caught Little Crow picking raspberries in his field and shot him dead. The Minnesota legislature paid the farmer $500 for Little Crow's scalp, then placed it on display at the state historical society.

By then, Congress had voided all treaties with the eastern Sioux. A year after the uprising, 2000 Santees were herded into a tiny reservation along the Missouri River, together with 3000 Indians from the Winnebago tribe, who had had nothing to do with the insurrection. The land was barren, with little rainfall and even less game. During the first winter, 400 people died of starvation and disease.

"The Plains are afloat in mysterious space, and the winds come straight from heaven. Anyone alone in the Plains turns into a mystic. Something happens to a man when he gets on a horse, in a country where he can ride at a run for ever; it is quite easy to ascend to an impression of living in a myth. He either feels like a god; or feels closer to God."
WILLIAM BRANDON

Opposite page: Following the Great Sioux Uprising, 38 Santees (three of them innocent) are hanged from a single gallows in Mankato, Minnesota, on 26 December 1862.

General John Pope. After his defeat at the 2nd Battle of Bull Run during the Civil War, he was relieved of his command for 'keeping his headquarters where his hindquarters should have been'.

1860: As the railroad began to creep westward, telegraph lines were erected alongside.

There never was a white man who did not hate Indians, and there never was an Indian who did not hate whites.

Sitting Bull

Shock waves from the Minnesota Uprising rolled westward over Dakota. As Santee refugees fled, 5000 soldiers plunged deep into Lakota territory, to punish Sioux and establish a new line of forts. At the centre of the resistance that rose up to stop them was a 32-year-old Hunkpapa Sioux war chief and holy man. White men called him Sitting Bull. His white opponents would later indulge in wild speculation about his origins – refusing to believe that any Indian could beat them so frequently in war. Some said that he was a white man in disguise; others that he could speak German and Chinese and quote Shakespeare and Melville, or that he had studied the tactics of Caesar and Napoleon at West Point. Everyone agreed that he was utterly fearless in battle and a genius at war.

As US forces struck deep into the heartland of Dakota, Sitting Bull rallied his people to try to drive the whites from their country. The 17-year struggle of one of the greatest leaders in American history had begun.

Following the campaign of 1864, Sitting Bull's band was in winter camp when runners arrived bringing horrifying news from the south. Disaster had overtaken their Cheyenne allies in Colorado Territory – along a little stream called Sand Creek.

To the prospectors and homesteaders crowding into Colorado Territory, one thing was perfectly clear: the Indians would have to go. Treaty commissioners managed to get some Cheyenne and Arapaho to move on to reservations, but most refused. Eager for any excuse to drive the Cheyenne from the territory, Governor John Evans took this as a declaration of war. In May 1864, he sent a fierce Methodist preacher-turned-soldier John Chivington into the field, with orders to 'burn villages and kill Cheyennes whenever and wherever found'.

By June, Chivington's brutal campaign had driven half the Cheyenne in Colorado on to the warpath – and given Evans the opportunity he had been waiting for to wage all-out war. In August, he got permission to raise a special outfit of Indian fighting volunteers to serve for 100 days. The 3rd Colorado Regiment was still being mustered, however, when peace suddenly descended on the territory.

On 28 September, Black Kettle – the genial 60-year-old principal peace chief of the southern Cheyenne – rode into Denver and asked for an end to the war. Evans was appalled. The tenure of his regiment was coming to an end and they had yet to kill a single Indian. Evans ordered the Cheyenne to withdraw to a stream 90 miles from Denver: Sand Creek.

At daybreak on the clear, frosty morning of 29 November 1864, Chivington and 700 soldiers bore down on Black Kettle's camp. When a junior officer protested that the Cheyenne were at peace, Chivington roared back: 'I have come to kill Indians, and believe it is right and honourable to use any means under God's heaven to kill Indians.' His order to charge woke the 550 sleeping Cheyenne and Arapaho in the village.

All was confusion and noise. The women and children were screaming and wailing. Black Kettle had a large American flag tied to the end of a long lodgepole and I heard him call to the people not to be afraid, that the soldiers would not hurt them: then the troops opened fire.

George Bent

Some men refused to join in. 'It looked too hard for me,' Captain Silas Soule wrote, 'to see little children on their knees begging for their lives, having their brains beaten out like dogs.'

In going over the battleground, I did not see a body of man, woman or child but was scalped, and in many instances, their bodies were mutilated in the most horrible manner. I heard of numerous instances in which men had cut out the private parts of females and stretched them over the saddlebows and wore them over their hats while riding in the ranks.

Lieutenant James Connor

Black Kettle and a few dozen warriors escaped the carnage, but before the day was over, 28 men and 105 women and children lay dead at Sand Creek.

I think Sand Creek was the saddest, most devastating event in the history of white and Indian clashes. It was a village that had hoisted the American flag and a white flag, signifying that it was a peaceful village. Yet a man who wanted to make a name for himself, who hated the Indian people for existing, went and attacked this village.

Mardell Plainfeather

'Colorado soldiers,' the *Rocky Mountain News* declared, 'have again covered themselves with glory.' Cheyenne scalps were strung across the stage of the Denver Opera House during intermission, to thunderous applause.

As word of the Sand Creek massacre spread like wildfire, the Great Plains exploded into warfare. In 1865, the Lakota, Cheyenne and Arapaho launched a combined military expedition against white settlements and forts along the emigrant trails. Cheyenne warriors rampaged across Colorado – burning ranches and stage stations, ripping up telegraph wires, twice sacking the town of Julesburg and threatening the outskirts of Denver itself. Despite everything, Black Kettle continued to try to make peace with the whites – before they destroyed his people entirely.

The Sand Creek massacre sparked outrage in the East, and bolstered the movement for Indian reform. In July, Senator James Doolittle of Wisconsin travelled out to Denver to plead the case for a peaceful solution to the Indian Problem. The choice was simple, he told the capacity crowd at the Opera House: either the Indians would be taught to support themselves on reservations, or they would be exterminated by the whites. 'There suddenly arose such a shout as is never heard unless upon some battlefield,' Senator Doolittle later wrote, 'a shout almost loud enough to raise the roof of the Opera House – "Exterminate them! Exterminate them! Exterminate them!"'

———◆———

For three-and-a-half centuries, Native Americans had fallen back before the advance of white civilisation. Now, for the first time in history, there was no place left on the continent for Native Americans to retreat. Between 1865 and 1869, as the crews of the Union Pacific and Central Pacific railroads began building east and west, the conflict between Native Americans and whites intensified.

On 9 April 1865, in the front parlour of Wilmer McLean's farmhouse at Appomattox, Virginia, Robert E. Lee surrendered to Ulysses S. Grant. The Civil War was over, and Union officers now turned towards the setting sun. They had reunited the nation North and South; the time had come to finish uniting it East and West.

Charged with the defence of more than 1.5 million square miles was the irascible red-haired major general, William Tecumseh Sherman, who had been instrumental in winning the war for the Union. He would be fighting hostile Indians, enormous distances, bad weather – as well as an angry Western press and public demanding constant protection, and an angry Eastern press, eager to blame the army for the least brutality to the Indians. He would also have to battle the government's shifting Indian policy, which wavered constantly between the peace pipe and the rifle. After inspecting the vast territory under his command, Sherman laid his plans:

The nomad Indians should be removed from the vicinity of the two great railroads, and localised on one of the two reservations south of Kansas and north of Nebraska. This would leave for our people exclusively the use of the wide belt of land between the Platte and the Arkansas rivers.

In August 1865, as Sherman struggled to gain control of his vast command, a vain, bombastic officer named John Pope launched the largest military campaign ever mounted against the tribes of the Great Plains. As thousands of emigrants prepared to travel west, Pope's armies moved out on to the plains of Kansas and up the Missouri River into Dakota. Meanwhile, three more columns pushed north into Wyoming – into the heartland of the Lakota Sioux.

———◆———

For a decade, the westernmost bands of the Teton Lakota had kept away from the main corridors of white expansion, roaming instead the rich, rolling plains of the Powder River country, far north of the emigrant roads along the Platte. Then gold was discovered in Montana.

Prospectors streamed across Dakota, but the fastest route lay through the last unviolated buffalo ranges of the Cheyenne, Arapaho and Lakota Sioux, along a road called the Bozeman Trail.

Steamboat advertisement of 1863.

Indian camp, Deadwood, south Dakota.

Determined to subdue the hostile Sioux and open the Bozeman Trail, Pope ordered the construction of a fort on the Powder River, then sent two armies deep into Lakota territory with orders to 'attack and kill every Indian over 12 years old'. The campaign was a disaster from start to finish. Plagued by bad weather and low morale, the cumbersome columns made easy targets for the fast-moving Sioux and Cheyenne war parties, which harried them relentlessly all summer. By autumn, hundreds of soldiers, already exhausted by four years of civil war, had deserted.

The government next tried bribing the Sioux, calling all the warring tribes into Fort Laramie for a council of peace, in the spring of 1866. Among the leaders in attendance was a shrewd 43-year-old Lakota warrior, Makhpiya Luta, whose name meant 'Burning Sky' or 'Red Cloud', and whose brilliance and fierceness in battle had already won him enormous prestige among the Oglala Sioux.

The talks began promisingly. In return for safe passage on the Bozeman Trail, the government promised the Sioux $75,000 a year and assurances that their land would never be taken by force. Red Cloud was about to sign when word arrived that the army planned to build two new posts, even deeper in Lakota territory. He stormed from the fort in a rage.

The struggle for the Bozeman Trail came to its first great climax in December 1866. All that autumn, Red Cloud and Crazy Horse had driven the army to distraction, roaming up and down the Trail, killing soldiers, and attacking troops near Fort Phil Kearney 51 times. Then, on the bright cold morning of 21 December, Crazy Horse and a small band of Oglala horsemen struck again, swooping down on a party of woodcutters not far from the fort. The fort gates opened and, with a company of 80 men, out rode an officer named William Fetterman, boasting that he could ride through the entire Sioux nation. As the soldiers approached, Crazy Horse and his band fell back – gesturing contemptuously from their horses, cantering back to taunt Fetterman, always just out of reach.

The trap worked perfectly. A little before noon, Fetterman's command followed Crazy Horse over Lodge Trail Ridge. Red Cloud – and hundreds of Lakota and Cheyenne warriors – were waiting for them on the other side. When reinforcements from the fort reached the killing ground, no one was left alive. Fetterman and another officer named Brown had shot each other in the head to avoid capture. Body parts were strewn for half a mile across the rolling countryside.

Lee surrenders to Grant at Appomattox, Virginia on 9 April 1865, ending the Civil War. George Armstrong Custer rode away from the farmhouse with the writing table, a present from General Phil Sheridan to his wife Libby.

Angered by the memory of Sand Creek, and by the prospect of any whites passing through their country, the Lakota and their allies took to the warpath.

The white men have crowded the Indians back year by year until we are forced to live in a small country north of the Platte, and now our last hunting ground, the home of the People, is to be taken from us. Our women and children will starve, but for my part, I prefer to die fighting.

Red Cloud

CHAPTER THREE

THE RAILROAD AND THE BUFFALO

1865-1869

It was one of the most rapid and astonishing transformations the world had ever seen. In just a decade and a half, gold and silver strikes had sent Americans flooding the Pacific Far West and deep into the interior. The number of white Americans west of the Mississippi had increased 40-fold – from fewer than 20,000 to almost a million. By 1865, stage coach lines and telegraph lines and emigrant roads had reached out across the wilderness to Denver, Santa Fe, Salt Lake City and beyond, cutting the continent – and the Indian domain – in two. Now the pace of expansion quickened, as Americans in numbers greater than ever before swarmed west – eager to finish the job of conquering the continent. Leading the way was the railroad.

The enormous enterprise required huge sums to get off the ground, paid for by lavish federal land grants and by the questionable financial practices of the builders themselves. But it worked. By 1866, the Union Pacific was advancing through Nebraska at the astonishing rate of more than a mile a day. Men flooded in from around the country and around the world to work on the railroad: hundreds of Irish workmen toiled along the Union Pacific line; and by 1866, the Central Pacific crews were almost entirely Chinese.

As the railroads pushed further out into the unsettled reaches of the continent, ramshackle tent-towns sprang up in their wake. Grocers, blacksmiths, pedlars and saloon-keepers crowded along the line to service the huge, rowdy crews. Most of the outposts collapsed as soon as the railroad crews moved on, but others remained long enough to sprout wooden buildings – a school, a church, a few stores – and began to attract a permanent population.

There was something about the railroad that gave the Native Americans a sense of how dire the end was that awaited them at the hands of industrial civilisation. The Sioux Wars were unimaginable without the presence of the railroad hovering in the wings. The word 'tamed' isn't strong enough in terms of what it did to the West – it's the thing that housebroke the West.

Tom McGuane

What the railroad was to the people moving west, the buffalo were to the people already living there: the condition of their existence, and their staff of life. The numbers were staggering – when the Teton Lakotas first came west in the 18th century, they found 75 million of the magnificent beasts roaming the Great Plains. With the horse and gun, the Lakota became lords of the buffalo, which became everything to them – fresh meat, warm robes, hides for shelter and battleshields, bones for weapons and tools, blood for warpaint, dung for fuel.

Then the white men started to come. The emigrant trails had already cut the immense herds in two when the railroads began pushing out into the buffalo ranges of Kansas and Nebraska. The demand for meat to feed the crews increased, and so did the demand for buffalo hides, which could now be transported cheaply and easily to markets in the East. Buffalo hunters galloped out to the end of the line, and the slaughter began.

In 1867, William F. Cody, a 21-year-old ex-Pony Express rider and scout, got a job supplying meat for the Kansas Pacific Railroad.

"It is incredible, the speed with which the national energies – released by the end of the Civil War – brought the West under subjugation in a matter of 25 years . . . It has to be one of the great population movements in world history – one of the great achievements in world history, if you avert your gaze from all that it cost in terms of human misery and environmental degradation."
ROBERT UTLEY

Left: 'The Sioux and Cheyennes are gritting their angry teeth because the Railroad is ploughing up their hunting grounds . . . ' – from the Kearney Herald, *17 November 1866.*

On the night of 6 August 1867, the telegraph wire at Plum Creek, Nebraska went dead. William Thompson and a crew of five were on their way down the Union Pacific line to find the break when they were ambushed in the dark by a party of Cheyenne warriors. Within moments, the crew was dead, and Thompson had been clubbed unconscious. He woke to feel his scalp being ripped from the top of his skull. Feigning death, he waited for the war party to move on, retrieved his bloody swatch of hair, and somehow stumbled back to Plum Creek, where he caught the next train to Omaha.

In a pail of water by his side, was his scalp, somewhat resembling a drowned rat, as it floated, curled up, on the water. At Omaha, people flocked from all parts to view the gory baldness which had come upon him so suddenly.

Henry Stanley

As tales of atrocity spread across the West, Sherman turned his attention to the central and southern Plains as 1867 began. Determined to protect the railroads and emigrants pushing through Nebraska and Kansas, he called on two of the army's most celebrated field officers: General Winfield Scott Hancock and George Armstrong Custer.

G. A. Custer, Lieutenant Colonel, Seventh Cavalry, is young, very brave, even to rashness – a good trait for a cavalry officer. His out-standing characteristics are his youth, health, energy and extreme willingness to act and fight. But he has not too much sense.

William Tecumseh Sherman

Shooting buffalo on the Kansas Pacific Railroad: wood engraving by J. Berghaus (1871).

A superb horseman and crack shot, he killed 4862 buffalo in under eight months – and won himself the nickname 'Buffalo Bill'.

They have run over our country; they have destroyed the growing wood and the green grass; they have set fire to our lands. They have devastated the country and killed my animals, the elk, the deer, the antelope, my buffalo. They do not kill them to eat them; they leave them to rot where they fall. Fathers, if I went into your country to kill your animals, what would you say? Would I not be wrong, and would you not make war on me?

Bear Tooth

Convinced a mere show of force would frighten the Cheyenne into submission, Hancock and Custer's forces fanned out on to the Kansas prairie, flags flying, drums and trumpets blaring. The Cheyenne could hear them coming from miles away. Unable to catch up with the fast-moving Indians, Hancock took to burning empty villages instead. By June, he had driven most of the Cheyenne in Kansas on to the warpath – but still hadn't engaged the enemy in an actual fight.

George Custer, meanwhile, had been conducting one of the strangest cavalry campaigns ever mounted on the Great Plains. Uneasy at being separated from his beloved wife, Libby, his behaviour became increasingly erratic. He issued brutal punishments for the slightest offence, ignored Sherman's orders to attack the enemy, and dashed off on buffalo hunts whenever the mood struck. By June, Custer's regiment had been out on the prairie for more than three months and had managed to kill only two Indians. When his exhausted men began deserting in droves, Custer sent a posse out with orders 'to shoot them down, and bring none in alive'.

General Custer is the most complete example of a petty tyrant that I have ever seen. I have utterly lost all the little confidence I ever had in his ability as an officer – and all admiration for his character as a man.

Captain Albert Barnitz

In July, Custer broke off the campaign entirely, and set off with two companies on a forced march across Kansas, to join Libby on the other side of the state. Two men were killed by Indians along the way, but Custer refused to halt long enough to bury them. One week after being reunited with Libby, Custer was arrested and charged with abandoning his command, shooting deserters without a trial, and inhumane treatment of his men. He was convicted on all counts, and suspended from his post for one year without pay.

❧

They came literally sailing, uttering their peculiar Hi! Hi! Hi! *and terminating it with the warwhoop – their ponies, gaily decked with feathers and scalplocks, tossing their heads high in the air, and looking wildly from side to side.*

Captain Albert Barnitz

On 26 June 1867, a party of 300 Cheyenne, Arapaho and Lakota warriors descended on Fort Wallace in western Kansas, where a company of the Seventh Cavalry was garrisoned. Seven soldiers were killed in the assault, including Frederick Wyllyams, a young Englishman and recent Eton graduate who had come looking for adventure on the American Plains. The English scientist William Bell photographed his countryman's corpse moments after the attack. No one in the Seventh Cavalry ever forgot what had been done to Sergeant Wyllyams.

I shall minutely describe this horrid sight, characteristic of a mode of warfare soon – thank God – to be abolished. We shall have no difficulty in recognising some meaning in the wounds. The muscles of the right arm hacked to the bone speak of the Cheyennes; the nose slit denotes the Arapahoes: and the throat cut bears witness that the Sioux were also present. I have not yet discovered what tribe was indicated by the incisions down the thighs, and the laceration of the calves of the legs, in oblique parallel gashes. Warriors from several tribes purposely left one arrow each in the dead man's body.

Dr William Bell

❧

After two years in the West, faith in a purely military solution to the Indian Problem began to falter. In October 1867, federal commissioners went out to Medicine Lodge Creek in Kansas, armed with bales of beads, cloth, knives and guns, and assurances that this time there would be peace – if only the tribes would move on to reservations in Indian Territory.

Chief Ten Bears of the Comanche protested, but in the end, he signed, as did Black Kettle of the southern Cheyenne and Kicking

In 1880, General William Tecumseh Sherman – named after the famous fighting Shawnee chief – said: 'There is many a boy . . . who looks on war as all glory, but, boys, it is all hell.'

Left: At the end of the 15th century, 30–60 million buffalo roamed across most of North America. By the 1880s, fewer than 1000 were left, two thirds of them in Canada.

Red Cloud, whose skill led to General Sherman's capitulation in 1868, died at the Pine Ridge Agency in 1909, having been deposed as Oglala chief 28 years before.

Mathew Brady's photograph of General Philip Sheridan, a brilliant (and foul-mouthed) cavalry leader and tactician during the Civil War.

Bird of the Kiowa. But when the commissioners moved north to negotiate with the Sioux, Red Cloud spurned them.

Finally, in the summer of 1868, Sherman himself came to Fort Laramie armed with a new proposal. In return for peace, the Sioux would be allowed to keep all of their territory west of the Missouri River, as far as the Big Horn Mountains – including their sacred Black Hills. In addition, the government would abandon its forts on the Bozeman Trail and designate the Powder River country 'unceded Indian territory' for as long as there were buffalo to hunt. No whites would be permitted to enter the Great Sioux Reservation, or the unceded territory, without the consent of the Sioux.

But after nearly two years of constant warfare, and two decades of broken treaties, Red Cloud was unwilling to accept mere promises. 'We are on the mountains looking down,' he said. 'When we see the soldiers moving away and the forts abandoned, then I will come down and talk.'

At last, Sherman capitulated completely. On 29 July 1868, Fort C. F. Smith was abandoned. One month later, troops at Fort Phil Kearney and Fort Reno were withdrawn, and the Bozeman Trail was closed to white traffic. After the soldiers had gone, Crazy Horse and a party of jubilant Oglala warriors swept down from the Big Horn Mountains and burned the forts to the ground.

And still Red Cloud refused to sign the treaty. That autumn, savouring his victory, he went hunting instead. Not until the first week of November did he appear, trailed by an entourage of warriors in war bonnets, to sign the Fort Laramie Treaty of 1868. Outmanned and outgunned, Red Cloud had masterminded the greatest strategic triumph in the annals of Indian warfare.

All through the summer of 1868, roving bands of Cheyenne warriors terrorised the settlers of Kansas and Colorado, killing 124 people. As winter approached, they began trickling back to the security of Black Kettle's camp in Indian Territory – to collect annuities from the government and rest up for the winter.

Following the disastrous campaigns of 1867, Sherman had replaced Hancock with his old colleague Phil Sheridan – an abrasive, hardbitten cavalry officer who swore almost continuously, and who believed, like Sherman, in the doctrine of total war.

If a white man commits murder or robs, we hang him or send him to the penitentiary; if an Indian does the same, we have been in the habit of giving him more blankets.
General Philip Sheridan

In the autumn of 1868, Sherman and Sheridan called from disgrace the one field commander they knew had the temperament, and the motivation, to destroy Indian resistance on the southern Plains. In October, before his year's suspension had come to an end, George Custer rejoined the Seventh Cavalry in Kansas, drilled them to perfection, then marched south into Indian Territory – determined to redeem his tarnished reputation. This time there would be no distractions, no delays.

On 23 November, the Osage scouts employed by the Seventh picked up the trail of an Indian camp, moving south over the snow-covered prairie. At midnight on the 27th, the regiment almost stumbled into Black Kettle's village, on the banks of the Washita River. Custer had no idea how many Indians lay before him, who they were, or how many were hostile or friendly. It was too dark to see the white flag of truce that Black Kettle had fastened to the top of his lodge.

In my mind, the battle of the Washita illustrates the ambiguities involved in warfare between the United States Army and all the Indians of the West . . . Black Kettle was the leading peace chief of the Cheyenne – there's no question about that – but Custer found his village by following the trail in the snow made by a war party of his young men returning from a plundering raid on the Kansas settlements.
Robert Utley

Dividing his regiment in four, Custer attacked the village from all sides at first light, while the band played 'Garry Owen'. But in the icy dawn air, the mouthpieces froze and the music stopped. As the Cheyenne rushed, panicked and screaming, from their lodges, Custer's men cut them down, firing and hacking at anything that moved. Black Kettle and his wife were shot in the back as they tried to flee across the Washita, and died face down in the icy water. The bloodshed was coming to an end when Cheyenne and Arapaho reinforcements began to arrive. Abandoning a portion of his command, Custer ordered his men to slaughter the 800 ponies they had captured, and had the bugler sound 'Retreat'. A reporter from the *New York-Tribune* compared the scene to a slaughter yard.

A few days later, Custer marched into Camp Supply with 53 prisoners in tow, boasting that his men had killed 103 warriors. In fact, only 11 fighting men had been killed at the battle of the Washita. The rest of the dead were women, children and old men.

They called it the battle of the Washita but there was really no battle. It was a massacre. From that day, the Cheyenne hated him, and joined with the Sioux to fight Custer. And when their scouts reported that Custer was coming, why, they were just anxious to get him.

Joe Medicine Crow

The battle of the Washita marked the beginning of the end of armed resistance on the central and southern Plains. All winter, the army harried the remaining tribes in Indian Territory. All winter, Indians straggled into Fort Cobb to surrender. When the Comanche arrived, one of their leaders introduced himself to Sheridan. '*Tosawi*, good Indian,' he said. Sheridan replied: 'The only good Indians I ever saw were dead.'

The Central Pacific crews had passed the northern tip of the Great Salt Lake and were heading east towards Promontory Summit,

where the two ends of the transcontinental railroad would finally meet. By then, Union Pacific crews had blasted through the rugged mountains east of Salt Lake City, and were pushing on towards the historic rendezvous. On 8 May 1869, the two lines of the transcontinental railroad finally met. Twin ribbons of steel now ran across the entire continent.

It's hard to overstress the significance of the completion of the transcontinental railroad in the conquest of the West. What it did was to bring a settlement of the American West, with a means of getting the products of the farm and the pasture to market that had not existed before. It tied the Pacific coast to the more settled East with rapid transportation. And, of course, the railroads, as much as anything, led finally to the conquest of the American Indian. It cut the great buffalo herds into two major herds and started the process of extermination.

Robert Utley

In the decades to come, four more transcontinental railways, and countless smaller lines, would be built across the American West, and wherever the railroads went, settlements sprang up. From Kansas to California, from the Yellowstone River to the Rio Grande, Native Americans were on the run.

Left: A celebratory photograph taken at the joining of the Central Pacific and Union Pacific railroads in May 1869. Engraving on the last, golden, spike read: 'May God continue the unity of our Country.'

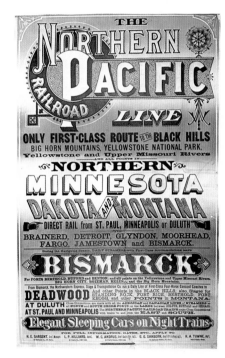

In c. 1875, the Northern Pacific Railroad was advertising 'elegant sleeping cars' on their services to, among other places, the Lakota's sacred Black Hills.

Left: Charles Schreyvogel's painting of the battle of the Washita neglects to show the Indians' white flag of truce or the dozens of Cheyenne women, old men and children killed by Custer's troops.

CHAPTER FOUR

THE WAR FOR THE BLACK HILLS

1869-1876

When the final struggle between Native Americans and European whites came, it began in the Black Hills of Dakota: the exact centre of the North American continent; one of the richest repositories of mineral wealth on Earth; and the most sacred place on the continent to the Cheyenne, Arapaho and Lakota Sioux.

Of all the promises made and broken during the long struggle between Native Americans and whites, none would cause more heartbreak and tragedy than the Treaty of 1868. Under the terms that the great Oglala war chief Red Cloud had fought so valiantly to secure, the Lakotas would be allowed to keep the Black Hills for ever – along with all of Dakota west of the Missouri River. They would also retain use of their old hunting grounds, the so-called 'unceded territory', for as long as the buffalo lasted. The treaty had scarcely been signed, however, when both sides began to argue bitterly over what it meant.

Red Cloud insisted his people had the right to trade and settle anywhere they wished, within the confines of the Great Sioux Reservation. The government insisted they settle on tracts of land far removed from any white settlements. White homesteaders, meanwhile, were outraged at the prospect of any land of value being set aside for the Sioux.

The white man writing the treaties never meant a word that he said. When we wrote a treaty that said, 'You will have the Black Hills as long as the grass shall grow,' we never meant that. It was outright lies. It was taking advantage of the Indians' naïveté, of their political unsophistication, and of their powerlessness in many cases. But the treaties didn't hold because one party to them never meant them to hold. It was simply a temporary expedient. It was criminal, in my own view, to lie to the Indians in the way we did.

Stephen Ambrose

In June 1870, as friction between the government and the Sioux increased, Red Cloud and 20 other Lakota leaders travelled east to Washington DC, to put their case before President Grant. For two days, they were treated like visiting heads of state, but the talks themselves came to nothing, and after two frustrating weeks, the delegation returned to the Great Plains.

Although Red Cloud had conceded nothing at the time, in the huge cities of the East he grasped for the first time the size and power of the white man's world. In 1871, he put away his war robes for ever, and reluctantly agreed to move to an agency south of the Black Hills, in Nebraska. Red Cloud's fateful decision divided the Lakota people. Many followed as he and other leaders abandoned the old way of life. Others refused to leave the buffalo ranges of the Powder River country. Increasingly, now, traditional Lakotas turned for leadership to such men as Sitting Bull, the chief holy man of the Hunkpapa Sioux, and to an enigmatic 30-year-old Oglala warrior named Crazy Horse.

Of all the legendary figures to come out of the West, none embodied the dreams of their respective peoples more completely than George Armstrong Custer and Crazy Horse. Although they had no way of knowing it, their lives had been converging for years. Their names would be etched for ever in the imagination of all Americans.

Vain, impulsive, hot tempered and brave to a fault, Custer had earned 726 demerits at West Point, graduating 34th out of a class of 34. His courage and recklessness were matched only by an uncanny instinct for self-promotion. No officer or politician in the 19th century was so frequently photographed – not Grant, not Sherman, not even Lincoln himself.

I think he's come to represent western expansion. You know, arrogance, nothing-can-harm-me kind of arrogance. It worked for him in the Civil War – the 'boy general'. It worked for him in Kansas, when he was fighting smaller tribes – basically fighting their women and children, he was great at that. But when he tried to take on some real men, he learned his lesson and he learned it for ever.

Mike Her Many Horses

"This is God's country. He peopled it with red men, and planted it with wild grasses, [but] as the wild grasses disappear, so the Indians disappear before the advances of the white man . . . Their prayers, their entreaties, cannot arrest the causes which are carrying them on to their ultimate destiny – extinction."
BISMARCK TRIBUNE, 17 June 1874

The 1875 delegation of Sioux chiefs to Washington DC to protest violations of the Fort Laramie treaty. Red Cloud said: 'God placed those [Black] Hills here for my wealth, but now you want to take them from me and make me poor.'

Opposite page: Glacier National Park, Montana: Indians starting off to hunt buffalo – a scene that would soon fade into history.

Two pioneer families take a break on the way west, c. 1870s.

An 1875 advertisement of the Burlington & Missouri River Railroad Company: the railroads bought land on either side of their lines and sold it to pioneers who were seen as potential sources of business.

The man who Custer would eventually face on the field of battle was the same age, loved war like Custer, and like him had, at a young age, risen quickly to become a leader of men. Introverted and shy, by the time he was 20, Crazy Horse had already become famous among the Oglala for his extraordinary skill in battle and his unswerving devotion to the welfare of his people.

But even they found him strange. He believed the world was made of shadows, that he could dream himself into the 'real' world that lay beyond. He threw dust on himself before riding into battle, tied a pebble behind one ear, and always rode naked except for a loincloth. But the Oglala tolerated his eccentricities because he brought them victory.

Nobody knows what he looked like because he didn't want to be photographed. He did not want his image to be taken by the white man. I believe that he didn't trust anything that had to do with the white man. Total and absolute resistance even to the point of not being photographed by this enemy people.

Mardell Plainfeather

These two men – Crazy Horse and Custer – had so much in common. They were both great riders. They both loved the hunt. They both loved the Great Plains – they were in a state of ecstasy when they were there chasing buffalo. And yet they were so completely different. Crazy Horses was in a state of being. He did not want change. He thought the life he was leading was the perfect life. He just wanted to be able to continue to lead it. Custer had that American quality of always being in a state of becoming. He was always reaching out for something in the future – more prestige, more power, more recognition. And Crazy Horse didn't want to be better; he just wanted to be.

Stephen Ambrose

———◆———

By 1872, the slaughter of the American buffalo had been underway for some time, and it would go on for the next 13 years. Most were taken, not for the meat, but for the skins, so many of which were shipped to tanning factories in the East that the price plummeted to 50 cents a hide. But the killing went on. A determined hunter could kill up to 60 animals a day. In one three-year period alone, hunters killed more than 8 million buffalo for their hides. The bones were collected for souvenirs, or crushed and sold for fertilizer at $5.00 a ton.

The hide hunters will do more in the next years to settle the vexed Indian question than the entire regular army has done in the last 30 years. For the sake of a lasting peace, let them kill, skin and sell until the buffaloes are exterminated. Then your prairies can be covered with speckled cattle and the festive cowboy.

General Philip Sheridan

A long time ago, this land belonged to our fathers, but when I go up to the river, I see camps of soldiers on its banks. These soldiers cut down my timber; they kill my buffalo; and when I see that, my heart feels like bursting. Has the white man become a child that he should recklessly kill and not eat?

Satanta

By 1873, the buffalo that had once blackened the southern and central Plains from horizon to horizon had all but disappeared. Less than two years later, the Kiowa, Comanche, Apache and southern Cheyenne would be forced to abandon the hunting life for ever and move on to squalid reservation lands in Indian Territory. Up in the Powder River country of Wyoming and Montana, one last great herd remained, but now that, too, was coming under attack.

By 1873, the huge crews of a second transcontinental line, the Northern Pacific, had reached out as far as Bismarck, Dakota, and surveying parties were pushing west up the Yellowstone River – into the heartland of the Lakota Sioux. Commanding the column of soldiers assigned to protect the surveyors was the dashing lieutenant colonel of the Seventh Cavalry: George Armstrong Custer. During the summer of 1873, forces under him clashed for the first time with those of Crazy Horse and Sitting Bull. For three weeks, Lakota and US horse battalions skirmished along the majestic banks of the Yellowstone River, until August, when, to the astonishment of the Lakota, the white troops and railroad workers suddenly withdrew.

Disaster had struck the white man's world. It was called the Panic of 1873, and it was brought on by the greed the West so often inspired in men. Reckless overbuilding on the Northern Pacific line had already brought the railroad to the brink of ruin when, on 18 September, the bank that had backed it went under. Within days, the entire national banking system had collapsed.

Once the rain of misfortune began, it didn't stop. Yellow fever swept through the Mississippi valley. Drought ravaged the Great Plains, followed by clouds of locusts that devoured crops and clothing and stripped houses of their paint. In places, the insects were piled so high that trains could barely move down the tracks. Before the disastrous year was over, more than a million Americans were out of work and the nation had been plunged into the worst depression in its history.

For years, rumours had been circulating of the vast mineral wealth that lay beneath the dark, forested slopes of the Black Hills. By the terms of the treaty of 1868, whites were forbidden to enter the hills, but as the depression grew worse, and calls for relief grew louder, all eyes turned towards the Sioux's most hallowed ground. Everyone knew that there was gold there – and in the summer of 1874, George Armstrong Custer was sent in to find it.

On 2 July 1874, Custer's mammoth expeditionary column – 600 soldiers, along with 110 wagons, three Gatling guns, four newspapermen, two miners and a 16-piece military band – marched west out of Fort Abraham Lincoln near Bismarck, Dakota. The ostensible purpose of the expedition was exploratory and scientific, but everyone knew that the real object was gold. On 27 July, while the expedition was camped at French Creek, company prospectors found what they had been looking for, and Custer immediately sent his chief scout galloping off to Fort Laramie with the news. One month later, the Seventh marched triumphantly back into Fort Abraham Lincoln.

By the spring of 1875, thousands of white prospectors were pouring illegally into the Black Hills. Red Cloud and other reservation leaders angrily demanded their eviction: 'The Black Hills is my land and I love it,' a Lakota song declared, 'and whoever interferes will hear this gun.' White prospectors, in return, angrily demanded that the Treaty of 1868 be revoked.

This abominable compact is now pleaded as a barrier to the improvement and development of one of the richest and most fertile sections in America. What shall be done with these Indian dogs in our manger? They will not dig gold or let others do it.

Yankton Press and Dakotaian

To give the invasion a semblance of legality, the government sent negotiators to try to buy the Black Hills for $6 million. Red Cloud held out for more, demanding cash and rations for seven generations to come, plus $7 million, but the white interpreter somehow mistranslated the sum as $77 million and the talks broke down.

Up in the buffalo ranges, non-reservation leaders such as Sitting Bull and Crazy Horse were pleased to hear of the talks' failure. 'I do not want to sell any land to the government,' Sitting Bull said, rubbing his fingers in the dust and holding them up. 'Not even as much as this.' From his stronghold at Bear Butte, north of the Black Hills, Crazy Horse agreed: 'One does not sell the land upon which the People walk.'

In Washington, patience with the Sioux ran out. In December, President Grant signed an executive order requiring all the Indians in the unceded territory to move on to reservations within 60 days. If they did not, the unceded territory would become a freefire zone, and a 'military force would be sent to compel them.' When the January deadline came and went, with no word from Sitting Bull and Crazy Horse, the Secretary of War received a simple dispatch: 'Said Indians are hereby turned over to the War Department for such action as you may deem proper.'

<hr/>

As the weather grew warmer, excitement and anticipation spread throughout the country. On 4 July 1876, the republic would mark its first 100 years, and there was much to celebrate. In just one century, the tide of the American Empire had swept across the entire continent from the Atlantic to the Pacific. The nation had grown from 13 to 38 states, while its population had swelled from less than 4 million to more than 40 million. It had gone through, and somehow survived, a bloody civil war. Now, even the last three years of economic gloom were being dispelled as gold poured in from the Black Hills to swell the nation's treasury.

Only one cloud darkened the republic's bright skies that year – far out on the northern Plains, where bands of Sioux and Cheyenne still refused to submit to the yoke of white civilisation. But even now the nation's forces were gathering to sweep the defiant Indians from Dakota, Wyoming and Montana.

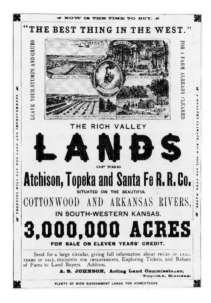

In the 1870s, homesteaders are urged to buy land in south-west Kansas – perhaps to take up residence in Pawnee, Comanche or Kiowa counties.

The womenfolk of a Mormon pioneer family at Echo City, Utah, c. 1869.

Cheyenne women making a buckskin lodge.

General Phil Sheridan's plan called for a three-pronged assault. One column would drive east down the Yellowstone. A second would move up through Wyoming, and strike the Indians from the south. A third column, led by General Alfred Terry and Custer's élite Seventh Cavalry, would march west out of Dakota and crush the defiant Sioux and Cheyenne.

As spring came, thousands of soldiers gathered for what most agreed would be the last great battle in the long war with the continent's original inhabitants. As the hour for the campaign's commencement approached, the officers and men of the Seventh prepared for war. On 17 May 1876, Custer said goodbye to his wife Libby. While the regimental band played 'The Girl I Left Behind Me', the Seventh Cavalry moved west out of Fort Abraham Lincoln, and headed towards Indian country.

———— ◆ ————

Something was happening on the northern Plains. All spring, the scattered bands of the Lakota and Cheyenne gathered to join Sitting Bull and Crazy Horse in the Powder River country. The great leaders came: Low Dog, Two Moon, Touch the Clouds, Little Big Man, Rain in the Face, Gall. For the first time in years, the movement of peoples down on to the reservations was being dramatically reversed, as thousands streamed north into the buffalo ranges – young men eager for war, family men with their wives and children – all galvanised by the presence of Sitting Bull and Crazy Horse, by their outrage over the invasion of the Black Hills, and by the promise of one last summer of the old way of life.

By June, Sitting Bull's camp had swelled to more than 1000 lodges, 7000 people in all, with more than 2000 fighting men. The buffalo were everywhere, and there was a wildness in the air. Seldom had so many Lakota, Cheyenne and Arapaho gathered in one place at one time. Never had they felt so powerful or so unified.

On 4 June, Sitting Bull moved his people to the valley of the Rosebud, and called for the Sun Dance to begin. It was one of the supreme moments of his life. The dance lasted four days. With his back to the sacred pole, Sitting Bull sat chanting and praying, while his adopted brother, Jumping Bull, cut 100 pieces of flesh from his arms. Then Sitting Bull joined the circle and danced for 18 hours, staring straight into the sun until, at length, a great vision came.

He saw white soldiers on horseback, riding just below the rim of the sun. They were upside down, and they were falling into the People's camp. 'These soldiers do not possess ears,' a voice told him. The prophecy was unmistakable. The Lakota had asked for peace, but the whites had not been able to hear. Now they would die in battle, falling upside down into the Indians' camp. 'These dead soldiers are the gifts of God,' said Sitting Bull. 'Kill them, but do not touch the spoils. If you set your hearts upon the goods of the white man, it will prove a curse to this nation.'

After the Sun Dance was over, Lakota scouts rushed into camp with news that white soldiers were approaching. It was beginning, just as Sitting Bull's vision had foretold. White soldiers were on their way, and the first strike would come from the south.

On 16 June 1876, 1000 soldiers under General George Crook were moving cautiously north along the valley of the Rosebud, looking for the camp of the Sioux and Cheyenne. They never found it. On the morning of the 17th, they were having coffee when Crazy Horse and 1500 Lakota and Cheyenne warriors came gliding swiftly out of the ragged hills and bore down on them in a full frontal attack. Even the most seasoned officers had never seen anything like it.

You can talk of seeing devils; there they were in full form, painted in the most terrifying manner, some with warbonnets adorned with horns of steers and buffalo. It was enough to strike terror to anyone's heart.

Private Phineas Towne

All day long the battle of the Rosebud raged. In the crumpled landscape of hills and valleys, organised combat was impossible, and the battle dissolved into a chaos of isolated fights – the kind of fighting Crazy Horse liked best. By nightfall, Crook had lost 84 men and had used 25,000 rounds. Unnerved by the ferocity of the Lakota attack, and short of men and ammunition, he retreated south to his base camp on Goose Creek and went fishing for the rest of June. The first wing of Sheridan's three-pronged attack had also been repelled. But the battle of the Rosebud had not been the fulfilment of Sitting Bull's dream. The big fight was still to come.

Chanting songs of triumph, and laments for the dead, Crazy Horse's forces and the rest of Sitting Bull's enormous village moved west towards the Greasy Grass River – a swift, shallow stream that the whites called the Little Big Horn.

CHAPTER FIVE

CUSTER AND CRAZY HORSE

1876-1889

Up on the Yellowstone River in Montana, the US Army waited for news of Crook's campaign, but none came. On 21 June 1876 – anxious that the Sioux would slip through their grasp – General Alfred Terry ordered a column of infantry into the field. Meanwhile, Custer's fast-moving Seventh Cavalry would pick up the Indian trail, then follow it west towards the Little Big Horn. On 22 June, the 611 officers and men of the Seventh moved out.

Custer kept up a relentless pace, 30 miles a day and more, pushing ever deeper into enemy territory. There were signs of Indians everywhere. Two days out, the regiment reached the grassy plain where Sitting Bull's Sun Dance had been held. Further up the valley, Indian scouts found scalps and beards that had been cut from Crook's soldiers and hastily tossed aside. An air of foreboding fell over the Seventh. Custer's favourite scout, Bloody Knife, implored his commander to proceed with extreme caution, but Custer's blood was up. A huge path of trampled grass, almost a mile wide, showed where the Indians had crossed the Rosebud, heading west towards the Little Big Horn, and Custer pushed his exhausted men on towards a line of low hills.

At dawn on the morning of 25 June, the Crow and Arikara scouts climbed to a lookout high atop the divide. They could just make out the Little Big Horn, 15 miles away, and as the light grew stronger, they gasped in astonishment. Even at that distance, they could tell it was one of the biggest Indian villages ever assembled on the Great Plains.

The Indian scouts began chanting their death songs. Bloody Knife warned Custer that there weren't enough bullets to kill all the hostile Indians now before them. 'If we go in there,' one of the white scouts warned, 'we will never come out.'

Custer shrugged off their concerns. 'The largest Indian camp on the North American continent is ahead,' he told his officers, 'and I am going to attack it.'

Oh, I'm sure that George Custer thought that he was going to ride through Sioux country and clean it up and be a hero. I have no doubt that he believed the story that he developed for himself. I don't think that he ever thought that, in a society as individualistic as Lakota people were, 7000 of them would come together for a war council.

Charlotte Black Elk

A few minutes past noon, the Seventh Cavalry started down into the valley of the Little Big Horn. It was then that Custer made a fateful decision. Already greatly outnumbered, he weakened his striking force still more – sending three companies under Captain Frederick Benteen off to the left. Then he ordered Major Marcus Reno and three more companies to cross the Little Big Horn and attack the village from the south. The rest of the regiment, Custer assured him, would give him their full support.

It was around two o'clock on that hot, cloudless afternoon when Reno's 140-man battalion crossed the swift, sparkling stream and turned right, picking up speed along the level flats, heading for the Indian camp. Once or twice Reno glanced behind him, looking for Custer – but he was nowhere to be seen. Without telling him, Custer had already changed his battle plan. Instead of supporting Reno's charge, he would ride north, screened by the hills on the east side of the river, circle the village, and strike the Indians as they fled. To all intents and purposes, Reno was on his own, and the dream-like sequence of events that would be called the battle of the Little Big Horn had begun.

I saw a great dust rising. It looked like a whirlwind. Soon a Sioux horseman came rushing into camp, shouting: 'Soldiers come! Plenty white soldiers!'

Two Moon

As the first bullets whistled through the tops of the lodges, the huge village exploded into action. While the women and older people snatched up the children and ran for their lives, the men ran for their weapons and their ponies. Sitting Bull, whose circle of lodges was nearest to where the first attack would come, rallied his warriors to defend their families, shouting, 'Brave up, boys, it will be a hard time! Brave up!'

> "The American character was formed during that period. The violence of the American character, the generosity of the American character. The greediness, the audacity all came from that period. And it wasn't all evil, but it was partly evil, and its effect is still going on. We can't get away from it."
> **DEE BROWN**

General Custer with his Indian scouts in the early 1870s, when he was in command of troops guarding the building of the Northern Pacific Railroad.

General George Armstrong Custer, photographed by Mathew Brady. During the Civil War, he had 11 horses shot out from under him. At Little Big Horn, it was his turn.

The battle of Little Big Horn as seen by Native American eye-witness, White Bird.

Crazy Horse, determined to outflank Custer's column, spurred his horse towards the far end of the village – away from where the fighting would begin – calling out to Oglala and Cheyenne warriors he passed along the way. '*Hoka hey!* It is a good day to fight! A good day to die! Stronghearts to the front, weak hearts to the rear!'

From high atop the bluffs on the east side of the river, Custer watched Reno's battalion thunder into battle. He would never know what happened: that Reno's charge would be quickly repelled as waves of Lakota warriors swarmed out to stop them; that Reno himself would lead the desperate retreat back across the river to defensive positions on the other side; that only the last-minute arrival of Benteen's column would save Reno's battalion from complete annihilation.

Looking on now as the battle began – still certain that victory was in his grasp – Custer sent back a messenger with orders for Benteen to bring up reinforcements as quickly as possible. Then, waving his broadbrimmed hat in the air, he shouted out, 'Hurrah, boys, we've got them!' and spurred his five companies towards the north.

———◆———

No one knows precisely what happened to George Armstrong Custer and his men. The events of that terrible, glorious afternoon would forever after be shrouded in speculation, fantasy and myth.

The column probably never reached the Little Big Horn. As Custer's advance companies neared a shallow ford of the river, 1500 warriors rode screaming across the shallows to stop them. Hundreds more leapt up from concealment in the ravines and gullies. It was probably then that Custer first understood the nature of his position.

He realised at that moment that he suddenly wasn't on the offensive any longer. He was on the defensive. The Indians had seized their moment. That didn't mean everything was lost. The infantry was still going to come up the next day. All he had to do was hold on in a defensive position and wait for the reinforcements to arrive. He had a wonderful eye for terrain.

Stephen Ambrose

As waves of Lakota and Cheyenne defenders countercharged across the Little Big Horn, Custer's men fell back, fighting all the way, desperately seeking higher ground. They were only a few yards from the top of the rise when they were hit with a final horrifying surprise: over the crest came Crazy Horse and 1000 Oglala and Cheyenne warriors. Rending the air with bloodcurdling war cries, the Indians swept down the ridge, crushing everything before them.

I could see warriors flying all around me like shadows, and the noise of all those hoofs and guns and cries was so loud that it seemed quiet in there, and the voices seemed to be on top of the cloud. There were so many of us that I think we did not need guns. Just the hoofs would have been enough.

Standing Bear

These soldiers became foolish, many throwing away their guns and raising their hands, saying, 'Sioux, pity us. Take us prisoner.' The Sioux did not take a single prisoner, but killed all of them. None was alive for even a few minutes.

Red Horse

No. Not like we envision it. Because of the Indian accounts: 'The soldiers broke and ran. Their knees hit their chins, they ran so hard, and we watched them for a while and shot them down like buffalo.' Not a last stand.

Putt Thompson

Some of Custer's men fought valiantly to the end. Some panicked and were cut to pieces as they ran. Some may have killed themselves to avoid torture and mutilation.

It took less than an hour for the sounds of battle to begin to subside. One warrior said later that the fight had lasted as long it takes a hungry man to eat his dinner.

———◆———

Dug in on their hilltop three miles to the south, Reno and Benteen's embattled men held out all through the night, and all through the long, scorching day that followed. Late on the afternoon of 26 June, the Lakota and Cheyenne began to withdraw: striking their huge camp, setting fire to the prairie, and heading south towards the Big Horn Mountains. The battle of the Little Big Horn was over. This had been the fulfilment of Sitting Bull's dream.

The next day, Terry and Gibbon's infantry column marched up the valley and into camp. They were stunned to discover the stripped, mutilated bodies of Custer's command, 225 men in all, lying in scattered groups where they had fallen. Custer's brother, Tom, was so badly disfigured that his body could be identified only by the initials tattooed on one arm. Custer himself had been shot twice, once through the left temple, and once in the heart. According to the army's official report, the body had not been mutilated. But Kate Bighead, a Cheyenne woman who had been on the battlefield that day, insisted the Sioux had cut off one of his fingers, then punctured his eardrums with a sewing awl – to enable him to hear better in the afterworld.

They tell me I murdered Custer. It is a lie. He was a fool and rode to his death.
Sitting Bull

It took eight days for word of the massacre to reach the town of Helena, Montana. It was not until the 4th of July that the first shocking reports were flashed by Western Union to newspapers across the country.

I saw Father coming up the street, his coat off, his vest off, his hat in hand, waving a paper, the old Tribune. *'General Custer's entire brigade has been wiped out,' he gasped. A great silence came over Monroe, then all the bells began to toll – every bell in the town. To this day, I never hear a bell toll that it does not bring back the memory.*

◆

Just six weeks after Sitting Bull and Crazy Horse's triumph, the homelands they had fought so valiantly to defend were gone. In July, General Sherman placed all the reservations in the northern Plains under military control, and 2500 recruits were soon pouring into Dakota, Wyoming and Montana, eager to avenge the murder of Custer and his men. Any compunctions about annexing Sioux lands vanished.

In August, Congress passed a law compelling the Sioux to sign over the Black Hills, the Powder River and the Big Horn Mountains, and move on to reservations.

Now the Indians were simply given an ultimatum: sign the paper or we cut off your rations. This was highly illegal. This was a blatant violation of the manner, prescribed by the Treaty of 1868, for making changes. But public opinion would now support immoral, unethical techniques to accomplish the end, because they were so angry over the killing of Long Hair [Custer].
Robert Utley

Forces under Colonel Miles harried the people of Sitting Bull and Crazy Horse without mercy. All through the winter of 1876, starving bands of Indians limped into Red Cloud Agency to surrender. By spring, even Crazy Horse knew the end had come. His people were sick and dying, ravaged by malnutrition, exposure and disease. In April, he sent word that, if he were given a reservation of his own in the Powder River country, he would surrender.

On 6 May 1877, one day after Sitting Bull and his Hunkpapa band slipped across the border into Canada, Crazy Horse – painted for war and carrying his Winchester rifle – rode into Camp Robinson in north-western Nebraska, at the head of a column of men, women and children that stretched for two miles. Thousands of Lakota and Cheyenne from the reservation lined the route, eager to see their great hero – to honour him, sing for him and cheer him on.

Tatanka Iyotake, known to white Americans as Sitting Bull. This photograph was taken in 1885, the year he spent with Buffalo Bill's Wild West Show.

Left: A buffalo robe painted with battle scenes, probably from 1871, after Red Cloud opted out of fighting and the Lakota divided, some to follow Sitting Bull and Crazy Horse.

An Indian village is forced to move. Undated wood engraving by T. R. Davis.

George Crook issued a warrant for his arrest. On 6 September, Crazy Horse allowed himself to be brought under guard into the army compound at Camp Robinson – lured in by assurances that he would be given his own reservation, west of his old lodge at Bear Butte. A crowd of Lakota warriors gathered on the parade ground as he passed through.

When the detail reached the guardhouse, Crazy Horse glanced through the open door and saw bars on the window, manacles on the wall and a ball-and-chain. He lunged sideways, struggled desperately to wrench himself free, and lashed out savagely with his knife. Little Big Man, who had ridden with him for years, pinned his arms tightly from behind. Someone called out: 'Shoot in the middle, shoot to kill!' Then an officer cried, 'Stab at the son of a bitch! Kill him!' and a soldier named William Gentles thrust his bayonet twice through Crazy Horse's side.

I wedged my way in between the guard and found Crazy Horse on his back, grinding his teeth and frothing at the mouth, blood trickling from a bayonet wound above the hip, and the pulse weak and missing beats, and I saw that he was done for.

Dr Valentine McGillycuddy

His old friend Touch the Clouds carried him into the adjutant's office. He would not lie on the army cot, but chose the bare floor instead. Near the end, his father spoke to him gently, saying, 'Son, I am here.' The wounded man replied, 'Father, it is no use to depend on me. I am going to die.' One hour later, the great Indian leader was dead. He was just 35 years old.

Three days later, Crazy Horse's parents placed their son's body on a travois, and started north, towards the badlands of Dakota. Somewhere out on the windswept prairie, not far from a shallow, winding creek called Wounded Knee, he was put to rest. To this day, the gravesite of Crazy Horse remains a closely guarded secret among the Oglala Sioux – who revere his memory and spirit more highly than that of any other leader.

◆━━◆◆━━◆

No tribe was spared in the tide of retribution that swept across the West after the battle of the Little Big Horn. In 1877, the Nez Percé, who had never killed a white man, were given 30 days to vacate

Crazy Horse tried to adjust to his new life, but there was no place for him in the surrendered world of the reservation, and in his heart, he knew he could never take up the white man's way. Jealous of the attention lavished on the famous warrior, Red Cloud, Spotted Tail and other reservation leaders did everything they could to turn the white authorities against him, spreading rumours that he was planning to return to the warpath. As the atmosphere of lies and intrigue thickened, Crazy Horse grew hostile and uncooperative.

In August 1877, terrified that the Sioux warrior he feared most would break out of the reservation and wreak havoc again, General

their Oregon homelands. For four months, the US Army pursued Chief Joseph's people across Idaho and Wyoming, through the wonders of the newly opened Yellowstone Park, and finally up towards Canada, where the Indians hoped to find refuge with Sitting Bull. They were intercepted in the Bear Paw Mountains of Montana, 40 miles south of the Canadian border and freedom.

In 1879, Colorado citizens brandishing the slogan 'THE UTES MUST GO!' brutally evicted the original inhabitants of their state. The Utes were exiled to a strip of land in Utah that the Mormons thought too barren for human habitation.

Two years later, Sitting Bull himself finally gave up the fight. He had hoped that his people would find sanctuary in Canada, but instead they had found famine, harsh winters, discouragement and disease, and after four years of exile, his once vast following had dwindled to 143 people. At noon on 19 July 1881, Sitting Bull and his followers, dressed in rags and on gaunt ponies, rode slowly into Fort Buford in Dakota.

In a simple ceremony the next day, Sitting Bull surrendered his Winchester rifle, not to a white man but to his young son Crow Foot – who in turn handed it to the commanding officer of the fort. 'I wish it to be remembered,' stated Sitting Bull, 'that I was the last man of my tribe to surrender my rifle. This boy has given it to you, and he now wants to know how he is going to make a living.'

The buffalo were gone now: scientists attempting a census in 1883 found only 200 of them in all the West. As what was wild about the West receded in fact, it grew larger in the imagination. In the same year, Buffalo Bill Cody started his Wild West Show – an outdoor extravaganza that dazzled audiences with spectacles from what already seemed like the *old* West: 'The Thrilling Ride of the Pony Express', 'Custer's Last Stand' and, as a finale, 'A Grand Buffalo Hunt on the Great Plains'. A huge success, it toured around the US and the world for more than 30 years.

In 1885, Sitting Bull himself was invited to join the show. Cody offered the famous Sioux chieftain $50 a week, as well as a $125 signing bonus and the exclusive right to sell his autographed likeness for $1.50 apiece. Sitting Bull got on well with his affable host, and enjoyed the attention lavished on him. But he was appalled by the squalor and poverty of the big Eastern cities, and most of his earnings, Annie Oakley recalled, 'went into the pockets of small, ragged boys'. When the season was over, Sitting Bull returned to the bleakness of his new life on the Great Sioux Reservation in Dakota – where a new onslaught against the Lakota people was underway.

For years, well-meaning reformers in the East had been insisting that, for their own good, Indians renounce their very identity as Indians and allow themselves to be transformed into hardworking American citizens. Now, at the Bureau of Indian Affairs, new policies came into effect, prohibiting Native Americans from practising their own religions, following many of their own customs and, in some cases, even speaking their own languages. Special schools were set up, on and off the reservations, to teach the Indians Christian virtue and Protestant thrift, and to inculcate in them 'the love of personal property'.

In 1887, to speed the process of 'detribalisation', the President was authorised to break up tribal lands, redistribute them to the Indians as individual allotments, and open what remained to white homesteaders. 'I would rather die an Indian than live as a white man,' Sitting Bull said, and bitterly fought any attempt to reduce the Lakota's land. But in 1889, over his opposition, the Lakota reluctantly agreed to split the Great Sioux Reservation into six smaller agencies, and signed away 9 million acres. 'They made us many promises,' a Lakota elder recalled, 'more than I can remember, but they never kept but one: they promised to take away our land, and they took it.'

William Cody received his nickname from dime novelist Ned Buntline and, before setting up his Wild West Show in 1883, acted in Buntline's melodrama The Scouts of the Plains.

Left: Buffalo Bill with Indian 'friends' in 1870. However, six years later, he allegedly scalped a Cheyenne at Warbonnet Creek, Nebraska.

CHAPTER SIX

GHOST DANCE

1889-1893

By 1889, it was clear to most Americans that the vast spaces, once seemingly infinite, were closing in. In the few years remaining before the frontier closed altogether, some Native Americans would try to dream, dance and pray their way back to the old way of life. But even that would prove too threatening to many white people. In the waning days of December 1890, 400 years of hatred, bloodshed and incompatible dreams would come to a terrible finale in the cold and snow of south Dakota, at a place called Wounded Knee.

❖

Just before dawn on New Year's Day, 1889, far out in western Nevada, a 34-year-old Paiute holy man named Wovoka fell ill with fever. During his delirium, the sky was darkened by an eclipse of the sun, and a great vision came to him. In it, God told him that he would rescue all the Indian peoples from the abyss into which they had been cast. An Indian messiah was advancing from the West. If the Indian peoples refrained from all violence, if they were virtuous and honest, and if they danced a sacred dance – the Ghost Dance – they would hasten the coming of the new world. Then all the whites would disappear, all the dead ancestors would come back to life, the buffalo would return, and the prairies would once more abound with game. In the winter of 1890, Kicking Bear, a mystic and former intimate of Crazy Horse, carried the gospel back to Dakota.

The whole point of the Ghost Dance was: those who are dead will return. And the weight among American Indians of friends and relatives who were dead had grown so great that it tipped the scales of the imagination. They knew more dead people than they knew living people, and they thought the dead would return. 'If we just believe hard enough, if we dance hard enough, all of our relatives will come back.' To me, it's a heartbreaking religion.

Ian Frazier

The Ghost Dance religion spread rapidly to reservations across the West – to the Kiowa, the Arapaho, the Shoshoni, the Cheyenne.

But nowhere did it take hold more powerfully, or with more tragic results, than on the desperate reservations of the Lakota.

The first dances began in August. In sacred ceremonies, performed as far as possible from prying white eyes, men and women came by the hundreds, then by the thousands. Adapting Wovoka's vision to Lakota custom, the dancers danced around a sacred tree, borrowed from the Sun Dance, which had been banned by the whites years before. They wore sacred garments called 'ghost shirts', which, Kicking Bear assured them, would render them invulnerable to white bullets. Joining hands, the dancers shuffled sideways in great concentric circles, the intensity of the dance increasing as they prayed themselves into a delirium, singing of the world to come. Exhaustion brought on rapturous visions of reunion and return: 'The People are coming home,' the words of one song said, 'the People are coming home.'

All summer, the Ghost Dance grew, spreading from one Sioux reservation to another, until normal life had all but ground to a halt. Fearing the dances would lead to war, the Bureau of Indian Affairs officially banned the ritual, but the numbers continued to grow.

Suddenly [there was] a fear that all these leaders who had fought these wars were still here. Sitting Bull was still here, Red Cloud . . . Many of these people that had been at the Little Big Horn, had been around the Powder River, were still here. Who knows what they would do?

Charlotte Black Elk

In October, Kicking Bear came to Standing Rock Reservation at Sitting Bull's invitation, to teach the Ghost Dance to the Hunkpapa Sioux. Sitting Bull himself never took part in the Ghost Dances, but he superintended them anyway, knowing that his people needed some kind of future to hold on to.

On 17 November, from his headquarters in Chicago, General Nelson Miles ordered troops to march on the Sioux reservations. On the 20th, the first units of the all-black Ninth Cavalry marched into Pine Ridge, and six days later, the Seventh Cavalry, Custer's old command, arrived by train from Fort Riley in Kansas. By early

I look off over the shore of my Western sea
Having arrived at last where I am
The circle almost circled
But where is what I started for so long ago?
And why is it yet unfound?
WALT WHITMAN 1819-1892

Opposite page: The Ghost Dance at Standing Rock Agency, Dakota, 1890, photographed secretly by Chicago reporter Sam T. Clover. Sitting Bull's teepee is on the right, and he is said to be the figure standing between it and the dancers.

The death of Sitting Bull, shot by Indian policeman Henry Bull Head in 1890 – given a true dime novel treatment by an unknown artist.

December, a third of the armed forces of the United States – the largest army mustered since the Civil War – was on alert. And as the troop build-up continued, thousands of Lakota Ghost Dancers, fearing for their lives, fled to the safety of a natural fortress in the Badlands, called the Stronghold.

As white anxieties fastened on Sitting Bull, James McLaughlin, the agent at Standing Rock Reservation, put a plan in motion. At dawn on the dismal, icy morning of 15 December 1890, 44 Lakota policemen on McLaughlin's payroll, quietly surrounded Sitting Bull's cabins on the banks of the Grand River, with orders not to let him escape. Among the arresting party were men who had ridden with Sitting Bull at the Little Big Horn and had suffered with him in exile in Canada. But the time of the holy man's power was over, and the Hunkpapas were divided into bitterly competing factions.

Now, they kicked open the door of his cabin, and brusquely told him that he was under arrest. His wife began to wail. Sitting Bull at first agreed to go quietly, but when the nervous Lakota policemen started manhandling him into his clothes, his fury rose and he began to resist. Outside the cabin, hundreds of Sitting Bull's followers had gathered. Now, as Lieutenant Henry Bull Head, the Indian officer in charge, pushed the struggling 59-year-old leader towards his horse, the crowd went wild, shouting, 'You shall not take our chief!' A warrior named Catch-the-Bear raised his rifle, and shot Lieutenant Bull Head in the side. As he fell, the policeman turned and shot Sitting Bull in the chest. Another policeman named Red Tomahawk shot the holy man a second time, in the back of the head. Then all hell broke loose.

For a few minutes, Lakota Ghost Dancers and Lakota police stabbed, clubbed and fired at each other at point blank range, before Sitting Bull's followers broke and ran. Almost as quickly as it had begun, the terrible struggle was over.

Sitting Bull's mangled body was thrown into the bottom of a wagon, along with the bodies of the dead policemen. Two days later, the Indian officers were buried in the Catholic cemetery at Standing Rock Agency, with full military honours. Sitting Bull's corpse, wrapped in a filthy piece of canvas stiff with frozen blood, was thrown into a makeshift wooden coffin and buried without ceremony in a pauper's grave.

Now time ran out for the Lakota Ghost Dancers. With Sitting Bull gone, many of his followers fled south, hoping to find asylum with Big Foot's band of Ghost Dancers on the Cheyenne River Reservation. Big Foot, who had led the dance among the Miniconjou Sioux, took them in, but he, too, was high on the army's list of troublemakers, and an order had gone out for his arrest. On the night of 23 December, fearing they, too, would be killed or imprisoned, Big Foot's band – 333 men, women and children – slipped quietly out of their village and headed south towards Pine Ridge Reservation, hoping to find protection with Red Cloud, the last of the great Lakota leaders.

General Miles immediately put three regiments into the field after them. As columns of heavily armed soldiers scoured the frozen prairie, Big Foot's people limped south. On 24 December, they reached the Badlands and, descending through a maze of buttes and gullies, continued south-east. Big Foot was now too sick with pneumonia to walk. Feverish and haemorrhaging blood, he rode in the back of a rough wagon, from which a white flag fluttered.

It was two o'clock on the bitterly cold afternoon of the 28th when a detachment of the Seventh Cavalry intercepted Big Foot's

82412

exhausted band. Although their orders were to arrest and disarm the fugitives, the short winter day was closing in, and scouts warned that any sudden attempt to take away the Indians' guns might lead to bloodshed. As darkness fell, Big Foot's people were taken under heavy guard to Wounded Knee Creek where they would be disarmed in the morning.

While it was still dark, the rest of the Seventh arrived from Pine Ridge. Four Hotchkiss cannons were placed on a little hill directly overlooking the Lakota encampment – which, by morning, had been surrounded by more than 500 soldiers.

Monday, 29 December 1890 dawned clear and cold. Colonel James Forsyth, the officer in command, called all the Lakota men to a council circle in the centre of the encampment, and ordered them to surrender their weapons. Anxious rumours raced through the compound. The Lakotas were being sent to prison or, worse, to Indian Territory; they were going to be killed – right then and there. Tension began to mount on both sides.

As soldiers began rifling through the Lakota tents, looking for guns, a holy man named Yellow Bird donned his ghost shirt and started to dance and sing. 'The bullets cannot penetrate us,' he sang. 'The prairie is large and the bullets will not go towards you.'

'Be ready,' one white officer warned his men. 'There's going to be trouble.'

Two soldiers began struggling with a warrior named Black Coyote, who refused to give up his rifle. Suddenly, the gun went off, and as the shot rang out, Yellow Bird threw a handful of dirt into the air. The white officers were sure it was a signal to attack.

As five or six Lakota warriors threw off their blankets and raised their rifles, hundreds of cavalrymen opened fire at point blank range. Almost half of the Lakota men, and many white soldiers, fell in the opening volley. Big Foot, struggling to rise from his blankets, was struck in the head and died where he lay.

The deadly gunfire at the council circle lasted less than ten minutes before the Sioux broke and ran towards a ravine just south of the encampment. As men, women and children ran, screaming, for their lives, the big Hotchkiss guns opened up, firing almost a round a second, the exploding shells shredding everything in their path.

Grandpa Beard said it was as if a huge canvas was being torn. The sound of the guns, and the sound of the bullets hitting people, the screams, the horses being hit, and the commands of the soldiers. And seeing the women falling, the men falling. The shells would explode and pick up the children and throw them – it was like they were being tripped. Hearing the horses screaming in pain . . .

Marie Not Help Him

Dead and wounded women and children and little babies were scattered all along there where they had been trying to run away. The soldiers had followed along the gulch as they ran, and murdered them in there. Sometimes they were in heaps because they had huddled together, and some were scattered all along. Sometimes bunches of them had been killed and torn to pieces where the wagon guns hit them. I saw a little baby trying to suck its mother, but she was bloody and dead.

Black Elk

Intermittent firing continued for several hours as soldiers pursued the fleeing Indians across the open countryside: bodies were later found as far as three miles away. Four of the officers in the Seventh that day had ridden with George Custer at the Little Big Horn, 14 years before. 'Afterwards,' Private Jesse Harris said, 'I heard remarks from the older soldiers. "This is where we got even for the Little Big Horn."'

Of the more than 300 men, women and children in Big Foot's band, 250 died at Wounded Knee. Twenty-five white soldiers were

Left: The Oklahoma Land Rush of 22nd April 1889, *painted by H. Charles McBarron. This exciting event signalled the end of the 'Indian Territory'.*

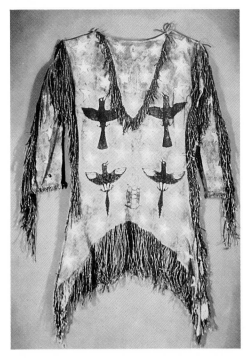

A buckskin 'ghost shirt' decorated with stars and thunderbirds, worn by an Arapaho in Oklahoma.

Opposite page (bottom): Big Foot, leader of the Miniconjou Sioux, after the battle of Wounded Knee, his body contorted by rigor mortis and the freezing cold.

A cowboy trail boss in Montana in the 1880s. Within decades, men like this would be displaced in the same way as the Indians.

Right: Guthrie, Oklahoma in 1893, four years after the Land Rush. In 1930, this area would see the discovery of a huge oil field and then, in 1934 and 1935, the drought that led to the migration of the Okies.

Opposite page: A photographer, starkly outlined against the snow, takes a picture of the burial party and the dead on 3 January 1891, after the battle of Wounded Knee.

also killed in the fight, along with 39 wounded – some by the Sioux, others caught in their own crossfire.

Out on the darkening field at Wounded Knee, the Lakota dead lay where they had fallen. It was not until 3 January, five days after the massacre, that the army finally escorted a civilian burial detail to the battlefield. Rigor mortis and freezing cold had twisted the bodies into grotesque shapes – Big Foot himself appeared to be rising from the snow, his arms reaching for something. Of the Lakota dead, 146 were buried in a single mass grave.

When I look back now from this high hill of my old age, I can still see the butchered women and children lying heaped and scattered all along the crooked gulch as plain as when I saw them with eyes still young. And I can see that something else died there in the bloody mud and was buried in the blizzard. A people's dream died there.

Black Elk

Two weeks after the battle, the last of the Ghost Dancers were coaxed out of the Badlands, and surrendered to the United States Army. On 15 January 1891, Kicking Bear laid his rifle at the feet of General Miles at Pine Ridge Agency. The Ghost Dance War was over.

Twenty-seven of the Lakota Ghost Dancers who had survived the massacre were sent east to prison in Illinois. Three months later, Buffalo Bill Cody helped secure the release of 23 on condition that

they appear his Wild West Show, which, the following year, added 'The Battle of Wounded Knee' to its stock repertory of exciting western theatre.

In 22 April 1889, after years of agitation by land 'boomers' and speculators, land in Indian Territory was thrown open to settlement by white homesteaders. At noon precisely, 50,000 prospective land owners raced frantically across the territorial line to stake out their claims – the Oklahoma Land Rush was on. The war of acquisition that had cost Native Americans their freedom and their territory continued as sheep farmers and cattlemen, cowboys and merchants, gunfighters and lawmen, ranchers and rustlers, railroad barons, big businesses and sodbusters battled each other for control of the land.

In 1893, Sitting Bull's cabin on the banks of the Grand River in Dakota was dismantled and shipped to Chicago, where it was put on display at the World's Columbian Exposition. At the fairgrounds that summer, a young scholar, Frederick Jackson Turner, rose to deliver a quietly momentous paper to a group of historians. He put forward two propositions: the experience of the American frontier had been the most important factor in shaping the character of the American people; and that frontier was now closed, for ever.

❖

In the 40 years following Wounded Knee, Native American land holdings across the West continued to dwindle, from 138 million to 47 million acres.

In 1980, the Supreme Court awarded the Lakota Sioux $105 million for the theft of the Black Hills – the $7 million Red Cloud had originally demanded, plus $98 million in interest. The decision was based in part on the document to which Red Cloud had triumphantly touched the pen 112 years before: the Treaty of 1868. The Lakota rejected the award, and continue to insist on the return of the Black Hills.

All America lies at the end of the wilderness road, and our past is not a dead past, but still lives in us. Our forefathers had civilisation inside themselves, the wild outside. We live in the civilisation they created, but within us the wilderness still lingers. What they dreamed, we live; and what they lived, we dream.

T. K. Whipple

RESOURCES

FURTHER READING

Black Elk Speaks by John G. Niehardt, University of Nebraska Press (US), 1979.

Bury My Heart at Wounded Knee: Indian history of the American West by Dee Brown, Arena Books, new edition 1987.

Cavalier in Buckskin: George Armstrong Custer and the western military frontier by Robert M. Utley, University of Oklahoma Press (London), new edition 1993.

Crazy Horse and Custer: The parallel lives of two American warriors by Stephen E. Ambrose, Penguin (US), 1975.

Creek Mary's Blood by Dee Brown, Arrow Books, new edition 1995.

The Custer Reader, edited by Paul Andrew Hutten, University of Oklahoma Press (US), 1992.

Eyewitness at Wounded Knee by Richard E. Jensen, R. Eli Paul and John E. Carter, University of Nebraska Press (London), 1991.

Five Hundred Nations: An illustrated history of North American Indians by Alvin M. Josephy, Jr, Hutchinson, 1995.

Fort Phil Kearney: An American saga by Dee Brown, University of Nebraska Press (London), 1971; Bison Books, 1989.

Frontiersmen in Blue: The United States Army and the Indian, 1848–1865 by Robert M. Utley, University of Nebraska Press (London), new edition 1989.

The Gentle Tamers: Women of the Old Wild West by Dee Brown, University of Nebraska Press (London), new edition 1989.

The Ghost-Dance Religion and the Sioux Outbreak of 1890 by James Mooney, University of Nebraska Press (London), 1991.

Great Plains by Ian Frazier, Penguin (US), 1989.

A History of the Indians of the United States by Angie Debo, Pimlico Books, new edition 1995.

The Indian Frontier of the American West, 1846–1890 by Robert M. Utley, University of New Mexico Press (US), 1984.

Killdeer Mountain by Dee Brown, Arrow Books, new edition 1995.

The Lance and the Shield by Robert M. Utley, Henry Holt & Co. (US), 1993.

The Last Days of the Sioux Nation by Robert M. Utley, Yale University Press (London), new edition 1994.

The Lives and Legends of Buffalo Bill: William Cody by Donald B. Russell, University of Oklahoma Press (London), new edition 1993.

Makin' Tracks by Lynne Rhodes Mayer and Kenneth E. Vose, Praeger (US), 1975.

The Nez Percé Indians and the Opening of the Northwest by Alvin M. Josephy, Jr, University of Nebraska Press (London), 1980.

North American Indians in Early Photographs by Paula Richardson Fleming and Judith Luskey, Phaidon Press, 1988.

Now that the Buffalo's Gone: A study of today's American Indians by Alvin M. Josephy, Jr, University of Oklahoma Press (London), 1985.

The Old West by Dianne Stine Thomas, St Remy Press, Time-Life Books (US), 1990.

The Oregon Trail by Francis Parkman (edited by David Levin), Penguin, 1983.

The Road to Disappearance: A history of the Creek Indians by Angie Debo, University of Oklahoma Press (London), 1979.

The Savage Mind by Claude Levi-Strauss, Weidenfeld & Nicolson/Oxford University Press, new edition 1995.

Son of the Morning Star by Evan S. Connell, Harper Perennial (US), 1984.

The World Almanac of the American West by John S. Bowman, Newspaper Enterprise Association (US), 1986.

The World Rushed In: The California Gold Rush experience by J. S. Holliday, Gollancz, 1983.

RECORDING

Sacred Spirit: Chants and dances of the Native Americans, Virgin Records, available as cassette (TCV2753) and CD (CDV2753).